# ISLAMIC
## FESTIVALS AND TRADITIONS

by Golriz Golkar

PEBBLE
a capstone imprint

Published by Pebble, an imprint of Capstone
1710 Roe Crest Drive, North Mankato, Minnesota 56003
capstonepub.com

Copyright © 2025 by Capstone. All rights reserved. No part of this publication may be reproduced in whole or in part, or stored in a retrieval system, or transmitted in any form or by any means, electronic, mechanical, photocopying, recording, or otherwise, without written permission of the publisher.

Library of Congress Cataloging-in-Publication Data is available
on the Library of Congress website.
ISBN: 9780756594411 (hardcover)
ISBN: 9780756594466 (paperback)
ISBN: 9780756594459 (ebook PDF)

Summary: Muslim people live all over the world, and they celebrate festivals and special days in many ways. Discover the traditions, celebrations, and histories behind Ramadan, Eid al-Fitr, Eid al-Adha, and more.

Editorial Credits
Designer: Dina Her; Media Researcher: Jo Miller; Production Specialist: Tori Abraham

Image Credits
Alamy: Imago, 20; Getty Images: .shock, 7, Maria Fedotova, 8, simon2579, 14, Ulet Ifansasti, 16, xavierarnau, 1, 13; Shutterstock: A Rehman 786, 29, Andaris Bangsawan, 21, Attitude, cover background (throughout), dotshock, 11, 23, Drazen Zigic, cover (bottom), hkhtt hj, 26, JOAT, cover (top), Odua Images, 15, ROZIblu, 25, Sony Herdiana, 19, yartthedesigner, 5

Any additional websites and resources referenced in this book are not maintained, authorized, or sponsored by Capstone. All product and company names are trademarks™ or registered® trademarks of their respective holders.

Printed and bound in China. 6098

# TABLE OF CONTENTS

Introduction to Islam ............................ 4

Ramadan ................................................ 6

Eid al-Fitr ............................................. 12

Eid al-Adha ......................................... 18

Life Events ......................................... 24

> Glossary ........................................... 30
>
> Read More ....................................... 31
>
> Internet Sites ................................... 31
>
> Index ................................................ 32
>
> About the Author ........................... 32

Words in **bold** are in the glossary.

# Introduction to Islam

Some people follow a **religion**. One of them is Islam. People who follow Islam are called Muslims. There are more than 1.5 billion Muslims in the world. Many live in Africa and Asia. But Muslims live all over the world.

Muslims have a **holy** book. It is called the Koran. They believe it contains God's words. Most Muslims are Sunni or Shiʿite. These are Muslim groups. They celebrate the same holidays, although their dates may be different.

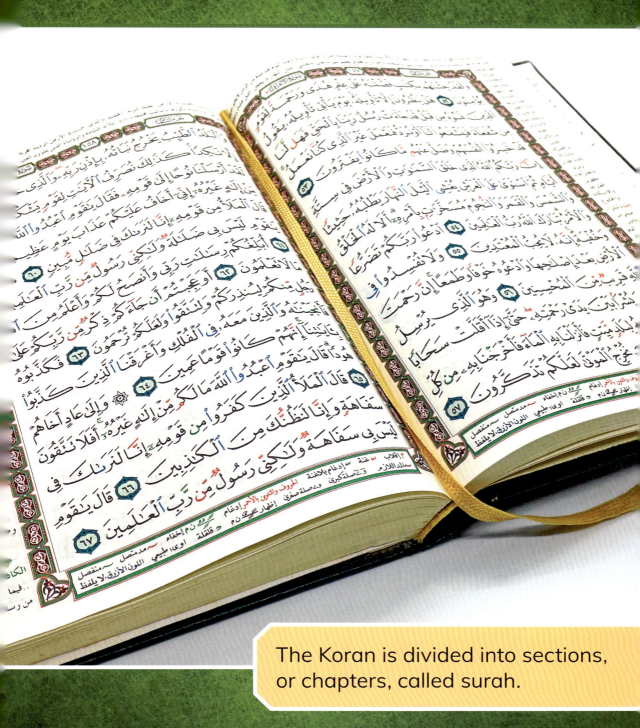

The Koran is divided into sections, or chapters, called surah.

# RAMADAN

Muslims follow the Islamic calendar. It has 12 months. Each month begins when a new moon appears. The ninth month is very important to Muslims. It is called Ramadan.

Muslims believe the **Prophet** Muhammad heard God during this time. God presented the Koran to Muhammad in a **revelation**, speaking the holy truths that all Muslims should follow.

Praying together is thought to be better for the spirit and the community than praying alone.

The first meal after breaking fast is called iftar.

Muslims **fast** during the month of Ramadan. They wake up before sunrise. They eat a meal. Then they do not eat or drink again until sunset. Even drinking water is forbidden.

Many people go to work or school. Some read the Koran during the day. They pray at **mosques** or at home. In some countries, a cannon is fired at sunset to mark the end of the fast.

Communities come together at sunset. They hang lights on the streets and decorate shops. Muslims who live in Africa and Asia often go out to eat. People enjoy meals together at restaurants. Dishes include stews and rice.

Some cities have shared community tables. Anyone can sit down to eat, and no one has to pay. Ramadan ends when a new **crescent** moon appears.

Uniting and gathering with family is important during Ramadan.

## EID AL-FITR

The end of Ramadan is marked with a festival called Eid al-Fitr. Celebrations last for one to three days. Some countries treat it as a national holiday. Muslims do not work or go to school. Some pray at mosques. Others pray at parks or beaches.

In North America, Muslims may not have days off. They must wait until after work or school to pray. They might gather at community centers for special events or large prayer groups.

Grandparents often host Eid celebrations for the whole family.

Special envelopes let children know a surprise is inside!

Muslims enjoy feasts during this festival. They share meals with their families. Children get money as gifts. Eid fitrana is a special payment adults must make before the end of Ramadan. Food and money are given to those in need.

Many Muslims decorate their homes with lights and decorations. The moon and stars are traditional Ramadan shapes. Some cities celebrate with fairs and parades. Fireworks light up the sky.

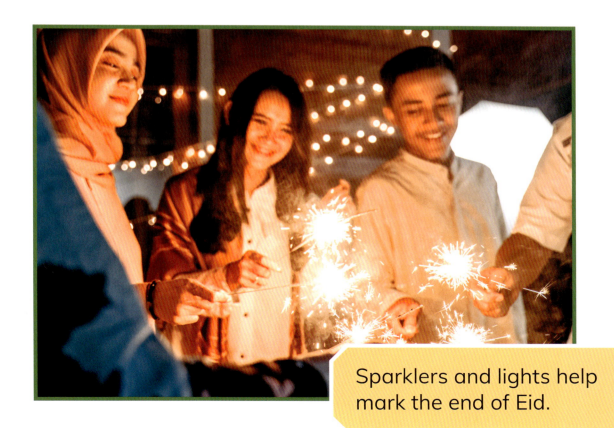

Sparklers and lights help mark the end of Eid.

Hundreds of millions of Indonesians gather to celebrate Eid.

Eid al-Fitr is recognized around the world, and each country's celebration is unique. People ride camels in Pakistan. Muslims in London, England, celebrate at a big park. Indonesians have a parade.

In North America, cities may have carnivals. Picnics are popular too. Everyone is invited to join.

## EID AL-ADHA

Every year, millions of Muslims visit Mecca during the last month of the Islamic year. Their pilgrimage to Saudi Arabia is called the hajj. Every Muslim must make at least one hajj in their lifetime.

During the hajj, Muslims visit the birthplace of the Prophet Muhammad. They pray together and meet followers from all over the world. They spend five days participating in **rituals** that remind them of their devotion to God.

Worshippers gather around the Kaaba, a shrine near the center of the Great Mosque in Mecca.

Henna is a dye made from dried and powdered henna leaves.

A four-day festival called Eid al-Adha is held at the end of the hajj. Eid al-Adha is celebrated by all Muslims. Schools and offices are closed. Many people wear new clothes. Women and girls decorate their hands with a special ink called henna.

At sunrise, people pray together at mosques or parks. Muslims in North America often pray at community centers. They listen to a holy leader who reads from the Koran.

Muslims pray in a mosque.

Friends and family visit each other. They offer gifts. They enjoy sweets. These include cookies and dates. A whole animal, often a lamb, is roasted. Dishes of meat and rice are enjoyed together.

Friends and family share the meal. They also offer food to anyone in need.

Curries, rice dishes, and stews are popular Eid al-Adha foods. However, flavors vary around the world!

## LIFE EVENTS

Birth is a special time for Muslims. The father holds the baby. He whispers prayers into the baby's right ear and then the left. The baby's first taste should be something sweet. The father rubs fruit juice on the baby's gums.

At seven days old, the baby's hair is cut and weighed. The parents buy silver that weighs as much as the hair. Then they give the silver to people in need. The family roasts an animal, such as a lamb. The meal is shared with everyone.

Shaving a baby's hair is a tradition for Muslims.

Muslims pray during funerals.

Muslim funerals bring friends and family together. A holy leader guides prayers. He talks about the person. He prays for the person to have a happy **afterlife**. Sometimes, women and children do not go to the burial. Instead, they **mourn** at home.

People visit the person's family after the funeral. Everyone shares a meal. The next 40 days are a mourning time. Muslims send food and flowers to the person's family.

Muslim weddings are big celebrations. Couples sign a marriage contract. They read from the Koran. Family members hold up a mirror. The groom looks at the bride in the mirror and offers her money as a gift.

A celebration then begins. Sometimes men sit apart from women and children. There is usually a large feast. Many Muslim weddings have music and dancing. Some weddings are one big party lasting all day. South Asian Muslim weddings may last several days.

Muslims are proud of their religion. They pray and celebrate with loved ones. They also help other people. Muslims honor Islam all year long.

The marriage contract tells the bride and groom their rights and responsibilities.

# GLOSSARY

**afterlife** (AF-tur-life)—a new life that begins after death

**crescent** (KRE-suhnt)—a curved shape that looks like the moon when it is a sliver in the sky

**fast** (FAST)—to give up eating for a period of time

**holy** (HO-lee)—having to do with God

**mosque** (MOSK)—a building used by Muslims for worship

**mourn** (MORN)—to be very sad and miss someone who has died

**prophet** (PROF-it)—a messenger of God or a person who tells the future

**religion** (ri-LIJ-uhn)—a set of spiritual beliefs that people follow

**revelation** (re-vuh-LAY-shuhn)—something that is revealed by God to humans

**ritual** (RICH-oo-uh)—an action that is always performed in the same way

# READ MORE

Abbas, Marzieh. *Ramadan and Eid al-Fitr.* Minneapolis: Jump!, Inc., 2024.

Andrews, Elizabeth. *Islam.* Minneapolis: DiscoverRoo, an imprint of Pop!, 2024.

Khan, Ausma Zehanat. *Ramadan: The Holy Month of Fasting.* Custer, WA: Orca Book Publishers, 2025.

# INTERNET SITES

*BBC: What Is Islam?*
bbc.co.uk/bitesize/articles/zrxxgwx

*CBC Kids: Ramadan*
cbc.ca/kids/articles/ramadan-be-good-to-yourself-and-to-others

*National Geographic Kids: Celebrating Ramadan*
kids.nationalgeographic.com/history/article/ramadan

# INDEX

babies, 24, 25

decorating, 10, 15, 20

Eid al-Adha, 20, 21, 22, 23

Eid al-Fitr, 12, 13, 14, 15, 16, 17

fasting, 8, 9
fireworks, 15
funerals, 27

hajj, 18, 20
henna, 20

Islamic calendar, 6

Koran, 4, 5, 6, 9, 21, 28

meals, 8, 9, 10, 14, 22, 24, 27, 28

Mecca, 18, 19, 26

money, 14, 28

mosques, 9, 12, 21

Muhammad, 6, 18

parades, 17

praying, 7, 9, 12, 18, 21, 24, 26, 27, 29

Ramadan, 6, 9, 10, 11, 12, 14, 15

weddings, 28, 29

# ABOUT THE AUTHOR

Golriz Golkar has written more than 100 nonfiction and fiction books for children. Inspired by her work as an elementary school teacher, she loves to write the kinds of books that students are excited to read. Golriz lives in France with her husband and young daughter.